Tartuffe

by

Moliere

Translated from the French by Harold Dixon

For royalty information, visit http://tartuffe.biz
or email info@tartuffe.biz

Tartuffe

Cast of Characters

Madame Pernelle	Orgon's mother
Orgon	Elmire' husband
Elmire	Orgon's wife
Damis	Orgon's son
Mariane	Orgon's daughter and Valere's lover
Valere	Mariane's lover
Cleante	Elmire's brother and Orgon's brother-in-law
Tartuffe	a religious hypocrite
Dorine	lady's maid to Mariane
M. Loyal	a bailiff
Police Officer	
Flipote	servant to Mme. Pernelle
Laurent	servant to Tartuffe

The action takes place in Paris, in Orgon's household
1669

ACT I, SCENE 1
Madame Pernelle, Elmire, Mariane, Cleante, Damis, Dorine,
Flipote

MME. PERNELLE
Let's go, Flipote. Let's get out of this place.

ELMIRE
You're walking so fast that I can't keep pace.

MME. PERNELLE
Don't worry, my daughter-in-law. I'll find
My own way out. Don't pretend to be kind.

ELMIRE
We gladly show you the respect we owe;
But, Mother, why the great hurry to go?

MME. PERNELLE
This household appalls me. No one in it
Pays me any attention for a minute.
Yes, I'm leaving your home unedified;
All my advice is ignored and defied.
There's no respect, everyone's tongue is free—
This house is a court ruled by anarchy.

DORINE
If…

MME. PERNELLE
You, my girl, are a lady's maid,
Too brazen and too lippy, I'm afraid.
You meddle everywhere, trying to be heard.

DAMIS
But…

MME. PERNELLE
You know what you are, my boy, in one word?
A fool. I'm your grandmother, I should know.
A hundred times I've told your father so;
That you were getting wilder every day,
And that you'd give him nothing but dismay.

MARIANE
I think…

MME. PERNELLE
My God! His sister, you act so discreet;
Butter won't melt in your mouth, you're so sweet.
Still waters run deep, but they're rarely pure;
You're hiding something by acting so demure.

ELMIRE
But mother…

MME. PERNELLE
As for you, my child, let me add
That your behavior is atrociously bad.
You set a poor example for them, too.
Their dead mother did much better than you.
You spend too much, and I'm distressed to see
You dressed the way a princess ought to be.
A wife, my dear, needs no such fineries
If it's only her husband she wants to please.

CLEANTE
But Madame, after all…

MME PERNELLE
As her brother, sir,
I love and respect you, but if I were
My son, her husband, I would make it clear
That I'd prefer you anywhere but here.
You preach a way of life to everyone
That decent people ought really to shun.
I've been speaking bluntly, but that's my way.
When I feel strongly, I must have my say.

DAMIS
Your mister Tartuffe is so full of speeches…

MME. PERNELLE
He practices precisely what he preaches.
And it infuriates me through and through
To see him attacked by a fool like you.

DAMIS
What! You want me, I suppose, to submit
To the tyranny of that hypocrite?
And we can't have any fun or merriment
Unless that fine monsieur deigns to consent?

DORINE

If we did believe in what he preaches
Then life would be a sin, so he teaches.
He controls everything, this zealot so bold.

MME. PERNELLE

And all that he controls is well-controlled.
It's toward heaven that he wants to lead.
Be more like my son and love him, I plead.

DAMIS

Oh, no. Not even my dad could compel
Me, grandmother, to wish that fellow well.
I see a showdown coming. I've no doubt
That he and I are gonna have it out.

DORINE

It certainly seems to me a disgrace
That a stranger took over things in this place.
When he came here, a beggar, he hadn't any
Shoes. All his clothes were hardly worth a penny.
And now he thinks he's in charge. He behaves
Like this house is his, and we're just his slaves.

MME. PERNELLE

Mercy me! Things would be so much better
If you just obeyed him to the letter.

DORINE

You see him as a saint in your fantasy;
But I see right through him. It's hypocrisy!

MME. PERNELLE

Watch your mouth!

DORINE

                    He and his servant Laurent—
I wouldn't trust either of them. I can't.

MME. PERNELLE

For his servant, Laurent, I have no proof,
But I'll vouch for the virtue of Tartuffe.
The reason you dislike him as you do
Is that what he says about you is true.
He condemns your flaws, for sin makes him burn,
And heaven's interest is his sole concern.

DORINE

Perhaps. But why just recently is it
He's upset when friends come by to visit?
Is heaven so wounded by all of us
That he should make such a terrible fuss?
I'll tell you what I think, between us here—
I think he's jealous of Madame Elmire.

MME. PERNELLE

Shut up! And think more about what you say!
He's not alone, at the end of the day,
To see all those carriages at your door.
Why, the whole neighborhood's in an uproar—
With so many servants yelling around
And huge crowds of guests trampling on the ground.
Perhaps in all this there's no real harm
But people talk; that's reason for alarm.

CLEANTE

But, Madame, why forbid them their chatter?
I think it would be a serious matter
If, because of what gossipers might say
We renounced our best friends and turned them away.
Even if we did that and closed up shop,
Do you think that that would then make them stop?
There is no way to stop slander, you'll find.
It's better not to pay them any mind.
Let's live in innocence as best we may
And let the gossipmongers have their way.

MME. PERNELLE

You all may chatter on and on all day;
But I intend to have the final say.
In taking in that pious man, my son
Did quite the wisest thing he's ever done.
I tell you, Tartuffe's truly heaven sent,
Since you've gone astray, to make you repent.
He gives criticism where it's needed
For your salvation; he should be heeded.
These visits, soirees, parties, and dances,
Are nothing but bashes where Satan prances.
Sensible people are driven half mad
By all these goings on - they are that bad;
A thousand cackles that add up to naught.
A wise preacher put it so well, I thought:
"Parties are like towers of Babylon,
For everyone there babbles on and on."

He went on at length to explain, saying…
To Cleante.
Oh, look at the joker, laughing and braying.
Go find your foolish friends and laugh your fill.
To Elmire
Adieu, Elmire, I've said all that I will.
More disgusted than I can remember when,
I do not know when I shall see you again.
Slapping Flipote
Let's go. Stop dreaming here, you stupid cow;
I'll slap some sense into you. I said NOW!
Move, you slut, move!

Act I, Scene 2
Cleante, Dorine

CLEANTE
I don't think I'll see her out.
I have had enough of hearing her shout.
How that old lady…

DORINE
Oh! It's a real shame
That she did not hear you call her that name!
She'd like the "lady," but it'd stop her cold
To hear that "lady" referred to as "old."

CLEANTE
She's so mad at us without any proof—
It looks like true love for her and Tartuffe!

DORINE
You think she's bad? Wait till you see her son.
You'll soon admit that he's the daffy one.
He used to be fine, but now he's dazed;
He sees Tartuffe and he's totally crazed.
He calls him brother, and holds him above
Mother, son, daughter, and wife in his love.
To Tartuffe his secrets will he confide,
He's his confessor and spiritual guide.
He pets and hugs him with such tenderness,
A mistress would be satisfied with less.
Tartuffe's the master and Orgon his dog;
Orgon smiles, and Tartuffe eats like a hog.
He gives all the choice tidbits before he's through;
And when he belches, cries "Friend, God bless you!"
In short, he's mad about him. He worships

Him, and hangs upon the words from his lips.
Tartuffe knows he's got a good thing going
And constantly tricks him without his knowing.
That holy manner pays him off in cash,
He plays his role with considerable dash.
And even that Laurent, his servant, strives
To tell us just how we should live our lives.

Act I, Scene 3
Elmire, Mariane, Damis, Cleante, Dorine

ELMIRE
To Cleante
Be glad you didn't come to the door.
She repeated all that she'd said before.
I saw my husband, but he didn't see me.
I think I'll go upstairs to wait to see
Him.

CLEANTE
Well, I'll wait here. I really must go.
I've actually only time to say hello.

Exit Mariane and Elmire.

DAMIS
Ask him about my sister's wedding, please;
I think Tartuffe's against it, and that he's
Trying to make my father change his mind.
That wouldn't be good, a change of that kind.
Valere has got to marry my sister
So that then I can marry his sister,
And I…

CLEANTE
Here he is.
Exit Damis. Enter Orgon.

Act I, Scene 4
Orgon, Cleante, Dorine

ORGON
Ah, my brother. Good day.

CLEANTE
It's good to see you back. But I can't stay.
How's the country? Is everything in bloom?

ORGON

Just a minute, brother, give me some room.
To ease my mind, it's important I see
How everyone's been doing here without me.
                    To Dorine.
Was everything all right while I've been gone?
How is everyone? What's been going on?

DORINE

Two days ago your wife had a bad fever
And a foul headache that wouldn't leave her.

ORGON

Ah. And Tartuffe?

DORINE

              Tartuffe? Why, he's doing fine.
Round, red, and rosy, and feeling sublime.

ORGON

The poor fellow.

DORINE

          She was nauseous that night,
And at dinner she could not eat a bite;
From her headache she could find no reprieve.

ORGON

Ah. And Tartuffe?

DORINE

          He ate alone, I believe;
And devoutly devoured, as I've heard,
A half leg of mutton and a game bird.

ORGON

The poor fellow.

DORINE

          Her pain continued strong
So she tossed and turned the whole night long.
Because of her fever she couldn't sleep;
It was a night-long watch we had to keep.

ORGON

Ah. And Tartuffe?

DORINE
        After eating, half asleep,
Upstairs to his bedroom he then did creep;
Got into his warm bed without delay,
And snored peacefully until the next day.

ORGON

The poor fellow.

DORINE
            At last and with some dread
She called the doctor, and then she was bled.
She felt a good deal better after that.

ORGON

Ah. And Tartuffe?

DORINE
        Needing courage, feeling fat,
He beefed up his soul at any cost.
To make up for the blood Madame had lost,
He drank with his lunch four large cups of wine.

ORGON

The poor fellow.

DORINE
        In short, they both are fine.
I think I'd better go upstairs and tell
Madame how glad you are she's getting well.
            Exit Dorine.

                Act I, Scene 5
                Orgon, Cleante

CLEANTE
Brother, that girl was laughing in your face;
And though you may say that it's not my place,
I don't blame her in this situation.
Whoever heard of such infatuation?
Is it possible that he's charmed you so much
That with the rest of the world you're out of touch?
You've relieved his misery, you take good care
Of him. But why must…

ORGON

　　　　Brother, stop right there.
You don't know the man you're speaking of.

CLEANTE

No, I don't, but I'm also not in love
With him, and I think you can judge men by…

ORGON

Brother-in-law, you'll be as charmed as I;
He'll enrapture you as only he can.
He's a man who…a man who…well, he's a man!
Follow his teachings and find a profound peace,
Reject this world, and see the rat race cease.
Under his guidance, I am not what I was,
He's taught me to reject love, because
The purest soul must be alone and free.
My whole family could die now and leave me
Like that, *(snaps)* and I wouldn't care at all

CLEANTE

What humane sentiments, brother; what gall!

ORGON

Ah! If that day we met, you'd been on hand,
You'd feel as I do now. You'd understand.
Humbly to our church he'd come every day
And kneel across from me and start to pray.
And he was noticed by everyone there
By the heavenly ardor of his prayer.
He'd sigh and weep and often with a spring
Of rapture, he would kiss the ground and sing.
And then when I left he would run before
Me, offering holy water at the door.
His servant, who follows him faithfully,
Told me of his dear master's poverty.
I gave him gifts, but in his modest way
He'd always try to give them back and say,
"That's too much! Half of that's enough for me.
I don't deserve all your sympathy!"
When I refused to take them back, he'd share
His gifts with the poor while I watched - right there.
Heaven at last made me take him in here
And ever since, how marvelous things have been here!
He protects my honor and guides my life
And even takes extreme interest in my wife.
Men look at her, and he tells me what they see,

And he's far more jealous of her than me.
You wouldn't believe the excess of his zeal,
The smallest sin is a danger that's real.
The tiniest offense fills him with dismay.
For instance, he blamed himself the other day
Because while praying he had caught a flea
And killed the small creature too angrily.

CLEANTE

Good God, my dear Orgon! I think you're crazy!
Or are you trying to make a fool of me?
In view of this nonsense, why do you insist...

ORGON

You're talking, brother, like an atheist.
You know that you lean that way in your heart.
And just like I told you right from the start,
Trouble's coming unless you change your mind.

CLEANTE

I've heard all the arguments of that kind.
If you're not blind, you're an infidel.
If you see clearly, you're going to hell.
What? Would you make no distinction for me
Between hypocrisy and piety?
Do you want to treat them all the same –
Honor the flicker just like the true flame,
Equating artifice with sincerity,
Confusing appearance with verity,
Shadow for substance; if that's not enough
Take counterfeit money for the real stuff?
Man, for the most part, is a strange creature
Who can't find the happy medium of nature.
The thought of moderation makes him laugh...

ORGON

Cleante, it seems you're too clever by half.
You're learned, brilliant, from all the great schools,
Compared to you, all other men are fools.

CLEANTE

I don't possess the wisdom of the ages
And I am not a learned sage of sages.
But there is one thing I know very well –
The difference between true and false to tell.
Nothing's more honorable in society
Than true devotion and zealous piety.

But I know of nothing more fallacious
Than hypocrites whose faith is baseless.
These sanctimonious charlatans with their
Histrionic and heretical glare
Betray real faith and make a laughing stock
Of the pious believers in the flock.
They pray not for grace, but money is fine;
Dressed like monks, they run back to Court to dine.
When they've an enemy they wish to libel
They use religion and quote the Bible.
These holier-than-thou types are all about,
But it's easy to spot the truly devout.
They don't sing their own praises; just the same
Their virtue is reasonable and humane.
They don't go around judging everyone;
They know that's arrogant and shouldn't be done.
Of preaching and sermons they have no needs;
They show they are Christians by their good deeds.
They don't pursue a sinner or reprobate;
It's the sin, not the sinner that they hate.
These are role models, people I admire;
Toward their example we should aspire.
And though you think that he's faithful and real,
Your man's not really the model of zeal.
You've been dazzled and tricked by him, I stress.

                    ORGON
Brother-in-law, are you quite finished?

                    CLEANTE
                              Yes.

                    ORGON
I am your humble servant.

                    CLEANTE
                    Please don't go.
There's yet one more thing. Valere, as you know,
Has your promise for your sweet daughter's hand.

                    ORGON
Yes.

                    CLEANTE
You'd even set a date, I understand.

                    ORGON
That's true.

                    CLEANTE
        But why has it been postponed, then?

                    ORGON
I don't know.

                    CLEANTE
        You're thinking of some other men?

                    ORGON
Perhaps.

                    CLEANTE
        Well, then, you're going to break your word?

                    ORGON
Oh, I didn't say that.

                    CLEANTE
                Has something occurred
That has made you want to lay down the law?

                    ORGON
That depends.

                    CLEANTE
            But why must you hem and haw?
Valere sent me here to speak with you.

                    ORGON
Praise be to heaven!

                    CLEANTE
            But what should I do?

                    ORGON
Whatever you like.

                    CLEANTE
            How can you delay?
What are your plans?

                    ORGON
            I plan, sir, to obey

The will of heaven.

                    CLEANTE
               Oh, yes, so I've heard.
But to the problem. Will you keep your word?

                    ORGON
Adieu.

     Exits
                    CLEANTE
          The lovers are in for a scare.
So, I had better go and warn Valere

                    Act II, scene 1
                    Orgon, Mariane

                    ORGON
Mariane.

                    MARIANE
          Father?

                    ORGON
               Come over here to me.

                    MARIANE
What are you looking for?

                    ORGON
               I want to see
If someone's there, trying to overhear.
It's a bad room for privacy, my dear.
Oh good, now we're safe. My dear Mariane,
You're a girl who's been just as sweet as you can,
Whom I hold dear and think most highly of.

                    MARIANE
I'm very grateful, father, for your love.

                    ORGON
That's well said, my dear; And to deserve it,
You must know my will and always serve it.

MARIANE

I like nothing better than to obey you.

ORGON

Splendid. About our guest, Tartuffe, what say you?

MARIANE

Who, me?

ORGON

You. Watch how you answer, okay?

MARIANE

I'll say whatever you want me to say.

ORGON

That's very wise, my dear. So, tell me, then,
That he is the most praiseworthy of men.
That he touches your heart and you'd rejoice
In being his wife, if that were my choice.
Well?

MARIANE

Well?

ORGON

What's wrong?

MARIANE
You mean…?

ORGON
What?

MARIANE
Forgive me, pray.

ORGON

What?

MARIANE
Father, who is it I am to say
Touches my heart and that I would rejoice
In being his wife, if that were your choice?

ORGON

Tartuffe.

MARIANE
            But that's not true, I swear it. Why
Do you want me to tell you such a lie?

ORGON
But you forget, I want it to be true.
My mind's made up, and that's enough for you.

MARIANE
You can't mean, father…

ORGON
                    Yes. Tartuffe shall be
United in marriage with this family.
He is to be your husband, that I swear!
It's up to me…
                        Act II, scene 2
                        Dorine, Orgon, Mariane

ORGON
        Sees Dorine.
            What are you doing there?
Are you so excessively curious
That you will risk making me furious?

DORINE
Around the house there's an ugly rumor;
Chance or conjecture, a small bit of humor.
You want Tartuffe and Mariane to be wed.
Of course that's rubbish, or you're out of your head.

ORGON
You find it so incredible?

DORINE
                    So much so
That I think your mind is starting to go.

ORGON
I'll show you whose mind is going, you crank.

DORINE
Yes, yes, of course. Enjoy your little prank.

ORGON
Dorine, I am not one to be baited.

DORINE
Ha!

ORGON
Mariane, you're going to be mated.

DORINE
Don't believe him. It's a hoax, a gag.

ORGON
I tell you…

DORINE
Your humor is starting to lag.
You can't fool us.

ORGON
I'm seething with passion.

DORINE
OK, we believe you, after a fashion.
But how can you who's been so judicious,
Who looks so prudent and so officious,
Be so stupid as to want…

ORGON
Shut up, please!
Little girl, you take too many liberties.
As master here, I won't stand it, I swear.

DORINE
Now, let's not get excited, sir. There, there.
You must be joking. Don't you find it odd
To think of Mariane married to that fraud?
He should be busy with fasting and praying.
And he brings nothing to you, I'm saying.
Why should a wealthy man like you select
A beggar son-in-law?

ORGON
What disrespect!
Speak of his poverty without a sneer.
His is a misery we must revere.
He stands above our pomp by his austerity

Since he has sacrificed his own prosperity.
All he cared for was heaven alone, so
He overlooked temporal things here below.
I'm going to help him marshal his forces
So he can regain his wealth and resources.
His lands're famous, their repute even higher;
You will see, he's a gentleman, a squire.

DORINE

Yes, so he says, and I think such vanity
Doesn't sit well with all that piety.
A saint whose spirit spurns this wretched earth
Shouldn't brag of titles and noble birth.
Real devotion seeks a low condition
Which will not suffer outbursts of ambition.
Why such conceit? But you don't like such talk.
Let's see if your Tartuffe can walk the walk.
Doesn't it strike you as a little grim
To give a girl like her to a man like him?
You must think of the consequences, sir.
Think about what this could do to you and her.
The danger to a girl's virtue is great
When she's forced to wed an unwelcome mate.
The type of life that your daughter will live
Depends on the husband that you choose to give.
Those horny husbands are the very ones
Who force their wives to be – what they become.
It's hard, in short to be a faithful wife
When your husband makes you run for your life.
It's hard for a wife to be true, I'll wager
If her husband is determined to cage her.
Give your daughter to a man she detests --
You'll learn father doesn't always know best.
Reconsider who should be Tartuffe's wife.

ORGON

And so you want to teach me about life!

DORINE

You could do worse than to listen to me.

ORGON

Let's not waste our time with this flummery.
Just trust my judgment. Oh, I know I said
That you and that young Valere could be wed.
But I hear he gambles, that little stinker,
And worse, I think that he's a free thinker.

And I have not seen him lately at Mass.

                    DORINE
Should he pray and bray loudly like an ass,
And kneel near you, to be sure to be seen?

                    ORGON
I've never asked for your advice, Dorine.
                    To Mariane
Tartuffe, however is so religious
Your blessings in heaven will be prodigious.
This marriage will bring you such joy and bliss
You'll never know such happiness as this.
You will be faithful in your mutual loves,
Just like a pair of little turtle-doves.
You'll never have fights or hostilities,
And you can make of him whatever you please.

                    DORINE
All she'll make him is a cuckold, believe me.

                    ORGON
What talk!

                    DORINE
          His sign shows it; the stars can see.
Against the power of his horoscope
Your dear daughter's virtue has little hope.

                    ORGON
Stop interrupting me. Quiet! It's wrong
To stick your nose in where it doesn't belong.

                    DORINE
I only butt in, sir, to help you out.

                    ORGON
So do me a favor you lout and butt out!

                    DORINE
If I didn't love you…

                    ORGON
                    Love me?   Oh, please.

                    DORINE
I love you, sir, from your head to your knees!

ORGON

Ah!

DORINE
            Your honor fills me with too much pride
To see you ridiculed on every side.

ORGON

You won't shut up?

DORINE
                I could never forgive
Myself if I let this misalliance live.

ORGON

Quiet! You impudent, brash little snake!

DORINE

What? So pious, yet what a scene you make!

ORGON

Yes, your chatter has made me mad, that's true.
And I don't want another word from you.

DORINE

So be it. But I can think, just the same.

ORGON

Think what you like; but just be sure you tame
That saucy tongue of yours. All right?
                To Mariane
                                    Now child,
I've thought everything through.

DORINE
                        It drives me wild
When I….

ORGON
        Tartuffe, is not that well turned out;
He nonetheless has…

DORINE
            A lovely big snout.

                    ORGON
He has other gifts which will coalesce
Into…

                    DORINE
          Oh, their life will be such a mess!
In her place, I wouldn't play the victim,
Before long he'd realize I tricked him.
He'd learn that night for the rest of his life
To fear the ready vengeance of a wife.

                    ORGON
So, you won't pay attention to my command?

                    DORINE
What? I'm not talking to you, Mister Man.

                    ORGON
What were you doing?

                    DORINE
          Talking to myself, that's all.

                    ORGON
Arrgh! One more word of this impudent gall
And I shall give her the back of my hand.
     *He puts himself in position to slap her, but
     Dorine stands immobile and silent.*
Daughter, you should approve of what I've planned…
This man I've chosen… as your fiancé…
     To Dorine
Not talking to yourself?

                    DORINE
          I've nothing to say.

                    ORGON
Just one more little word?

                    DORINE
          No thanks, I'll pass.

                    ORGON
I'm waiting for you.

                    DORINE
          I'm not such an ass.

ORGON

In short, my girl, you must marry the man
I've chosen for you and respect my plan.

DORINE

I'd never marry him in a million years!

ORGON

That handmaid of yours will bring me to tears!
Her flippant, cheeky words have got me so
Excited, and I'm certainly in no
Condition to finish our little talk.
To calm myself, I'm going out for a walk.
                    Exits.
                        Act II, scene 3
                        Mariane, Dorine

DORINE

Well, has the cat got your tongue? Must I play
Your part in this and say what you should say?
You let him propose a project so absurd
Yet you haven't answered with a single word.

MARIANE

What can I do? My father is the master.

DORINE

Do anything to stop such a disaster.

MARIANE

What?

DORINE

    Tell him that his way looks rather grim,
And that you'll marry for yourself, not him.
You're the one that's going to be the bride,
So it's you, not him, who should be satisfied.
Since his Tartuffe is above correction,
He can marry him without objection.

MARIANE

Father is always so powerful. I fear
That I could never oppose him. Oh, dear!

DORINE

Valere loves you. Now, let's reason together.

Do you love him, for now and forever?

                    MARIANE
Ah! What an injustice! What a suggestion!
You've no reason to even ask that question!
I've told you a hundred times how I adore him.
You know the depth of my passion for him.

                    DORINE
How do I know you're saying what you feel,
And that this passion for Valere is real?

                    MARIANE
Ah! You do me a great wrong to doubt it.
You know I've been too open about it.

                    DORINE
You love him then.

                    MARIANE
          Yes, with a burning flame!

                    DORINE
And he, I take it, loves you just the same?

                    MARIANE
I think so.

                    DORINE
          And Valere is just as hot
For this marriage as you?

                    MARIANE
               I won't say not!

                    DORINE
About this other match, what is your plan?

                    MARIANE
I'll kill myself before marrying that man.

                    DORINE
Oh, I had not thought of that. How splendid!
Just die, and all your troubles will be ended.
A marvelous idea! Oh, it drives me wild
When I hear her talk like a silly child.

MARIANE

Goodness, Dorine! That's so harsh! You don't feel
Any pity for my despair that's so real.

DORINE

I've no sympathy when you get this dizzy.
Tartuffe's not giving up so easily, is he?

MARIANE

What can I do? You know how shy I get.

DORINE

True love needs a heart strong and passionate.

MARIANE

My love for Valere's the same I've always had,
But shouldn't he be the one to deal with Dad?

DORINE

What? If your father is so crazed and aloof
And so infatuated with his Tartuffe
That all your wedding plans are up in the air,
How's that possibly the fault of Valere?

MARIANE

If I defy my father and act that mean,
Won't my deep love for Valere be seen?
Shall I give up, for his charm and beauty,
My modesty, which is a woman's duty?
Shall I declare my love to the world and flaunt…

DORINE

No, don't do anything. I see you want
To be Madame Tartuffe. It would be wrong
For me to divert a desire so strong.
What right do I have to oppose your wish?
Just look at Tartuffe – he is quite a dish.
With that pink complexion, those big red ears,
Think what pleasure you'll have over the years.

MARIANE

Good lord!

DORINE

Your soul will know eternal bliss
Wedded to such an ideal man as this.

                    MARIANE
You've got to stop talking like that, Dorine.
Try to be helpful. Stop being so mean.
That's enough. I give in. Tell me what to do.

                    DORINE
No. A daughter must to her father be true,
Even if he gives her to a chimpanzee.
You can't complain. Oh, the things I can see
In the life that you'll live...

                    MARIANE
                         You're killing me.
I need your help and not this mockery.

                    DORINE
Your servant, mam'selle.

                    MARIANE
                    Oh, please, Dorine dear.

                    DORINE
This marriage must go through as planned, I fear.

                    MARIANE
Dorine...

                    DORINE
          No.

                    MARIANE
          What if I say that I will...

                    DORINE
No. Tartuffe's your man, and you shall have your
fill.

                    MARIANE
You know that in you I've always confided...

                    DORINE
No. You're going to be tartuffefided.

                    MARIANE
All right. As long as you refuse to care,
Leave me alone, henceforth, with my despair.
This gloom will be wherever my heart goes;

I have one certain remedy for my woes.

                    DORINE
Alright, come back. I'm not mad any more.
You need some pity for what is in store.

                    MARIANE
If they make me swallow this bitter pill,
I tell you that I shall just die, I will.

                    DORINE
Don't worry. We'll devise some plan or other
To stop him. But here's Valere, your lover.

                    Act II, scene 4
                    Valere, Mariane, Dorine

                    VALERE
Mademoiselle, there's a rumor going round
That's news to me; I wonder if it's sound.

                    MARIANE
What?

                    VALERE
     That you're marrying Tartuffe.

                    MARIANE
                              Indeed,
That is what my father has just decreed.

                    VALERE
Your father, mademoiselle…

                    MARIANE
                    Has changed his mind,
And has promised me to Tartuffe, I find.

                    VALERE
You can't be serious.

                    MARIANE
              Oh, yes, I can.
He's got his heart firmly set upon the plan.

                    VALERE
And what do you plan to do, this being so,
Mariane?

                    MARIANE
          I do not know.

                    VALERE
               You don't know?
          Aside.
She's honest.

                    MARIANE
          No.

                    VALERE
          No?

                    MARIANE
               What do you advise?

                    VALERE
Well, I say marry him. That would be wise.

                    MARIANE
That's your advice?

                    VALERE
          Yes.

                    MARIANE
               Really?

                    VALERE
                         Oh, indeed.
This is a glorious choice that you should heed.

                    MARIANE
Thank you very much for the suggestion.

                    VALERE
I'm sure you'll follow it without question.

                    MARIANE
It didn't break your heart to give it, my dear.

                    VALERE
I told you, Mam'selle, what you wanted to hear.

                    MARIANE
And I will do what you want me to do.

                    DORINE
Let's see what this affair is coming to.
                Withdraws upstage

                    VALERE
So! I mean nothing to you. I can't believe
Anything you said…

                    MARIANE
                Enough of that, please.
You have told me plainly that I should wed
The man that father has got in his head.
And since you've given me such good advice,
I'll marry the man without thinking twice.

                    VALERE
Oh, no. Your decision was already made
Before I'd even uttered a sound.   You've played
With love harshly. You're seizing an absurd
Pretext to excuse the breaking of your word.

                    MARIANE
That's true. Well said.

                    VALERE
                No doubt. And in your heart
You've never really loved me from the start.

                    MARIANE
Alas! You're free to think that if you choose.

                    VALERE
Yes, that's what I think. I've nothing to lose.
You think you've wounded me, but I know where
To find someone else who'll love me, so there.

                    MARIANE
I'm sure you do, because your good qualities
Inspire affection…

VALERE
                    Forget my qualities, please.
Your conduct shows they don't inspire you.
But there's someone else now that we are through,
And I know she won't think it a disgrace
To compensate my loss and take your place.

MARIANE
I'm no great loss. You'll find consolation
In those new arms without hesitation.

VALERE
Yes, I'll do my best to go on, that's true.
You've rejected me, I must forget you.
Or if I can't forget, I shall pretend.
Time and pain will help me achieve this end.
It seems to be inexcusably weak
To go on loving when one is obsolete.

MARIANE
What a lofty, noble inspiration.

VALERE
And one that deserves our consideration.
What? Would you like it better if I never
Gave you up and just loved you forever?
Should I watch a rival hold you in his arms
And not comfort my heart with other charms?

MARIANE
On the contrary, that's just what I'd like.
I want you to leave. Go on. Take a hike.

VALERE
You want me to?

MARIANE
          Yes.

VALERE
                         Insults in profusion!
I shall leave now without further confusion.
                    Starts to go.

MARIANE
Very well.

                    VALERE
          Remember at least that it's you
Who's forcing my heart into what I'll do.

                    MARIANE
Yes.

                    VALERE
                Coming back.
          All I'm doing is, as I see it,
Following your example.

                    MARIANE
                    So be it.
                    VALERE
                Leaving.
Enough. I'll carry out your wishes, then.

                    MARIANE
Very good.

                    VALERE
                Coming back.
          You'll never see me again.

                    MARIANE
Excellent.

                    VALERE
            *Walking to the door, then turning
            around.*
          Huh?

                    MARIANE
            What?

                    VALERE
            Did you call my name?

                    MARIANE
Who, me? You're dreaming.

                    VALERE
            I won't play this game.
Adieu, Mademoiselle.
                Goes away slowly.

MARIANE
Adieu, Monsieur.

DORINE
                              Me,
I find them both as mad as mad can be.
I've let you throw these insults to and fro
To see just how far this squabbling would go.
                Grabbing Valere by the arm.
Hey! Valere!

VALERE
Pretending to resist.
What do you want?

DORINE
                    What's your hurry?
Come here.

VALERE
        No, no. She's put me in a fury.
Don't hold me back. I'll do what she's decreed.

DORINE
Stand still.

VALERE
        It's too late now. We've both agreed.

DORINE
Ah!

MARIANE
        Aside.
I can tell he hates the sight of me.
So, I'll leave and give him his liberty.

DORINE
        Leaves Valere, runs to Mariane.
Oh, no. Now you.

MARIANE
Let go.

DORINE
                    Come on.

MARIANE

                                        Alack,
Nothing you can say will make me come back.

VALERE
                Aside.
I see it's torturing her to look at me.
No doubt I should leave, and thus set her free.

DORINE
            Leaves Mariane, runs to Valere
Not you again! The devil take you two!
Now stop this nonsense. Come here, both of you.

VALERE
What's the point of this?

MARIANE
                What do you desire?

DORINE
I'm going to arrange a little ceasefire.
                To Valere.
Why in the world did you make all this fuss?

VALERE
She was the one acting crazy, I trust.

DORINE
It was wild how you over reacted.

MARIANE
Did you not see how badly he acted?

DORINE
Fools on both sides.
                To Valere.
                Valere, her desire
Is to love only you; her heart is on fire.
                To Mariane.
He loves only you, and wants no other wife
But you, Mariane, I swear on my life.

MARIANE
But why offer me such a bad opinion?

                    VALERE
Why must she act like such a little minion?

                    DORINE
You're both crazy. Now here, give me your hand.
                    To Valere.
Let's go.
                    VALERE
          What for?

                    DORINE
                There.
          To Mariane.
                    Come on, I know you can.

                    MARIANE
What does all this mean?

                    DORINE
                Come on now, let's go.
You love each other better than you know.

                    VALERE
Don't be so reluctant. Do you think you can
Look at a man tenderly, dear Mariane?

                    DORINE
To tell you the truth, lovers are insane.

                    VALERE
But really, don't I have reason to complain?
And you must admit that you were naughty
To enjoy hurting me and acting haughty.

                    MARIANE
But you, aren't you the most ungrateful man...?

                    DORINE
Let's postpone this argument, if we can.
To stop this marriage we've got to connive.

                    MARIANE
Tell us what secret plans we can contrive.

                    DORINE
What we've got to do is come up with a trick.
Your father's weird; He's never been so thick.

But you two must, even though it seems wrong,
Pretend to agree with him, just go along.
That will buy us some time; but now we've got
To get out of here, before we get caught.
                    To Valere.
Go find your friends, and tell them, if they can,
To pressure her father to give up his plan.
                    To Mariane.
We will enlist the efforts of your brother
And also ask the aid of your stepmother.
                    To Valere.
Adieu.

                    VALERE
    Whatever the rest of us may do,
My greatest hope, dear, is truly in you.

                    MARIANE
My devotion is not my father's affair;
I'll never be with anyone but Valere.

                    VALERE
How happy you've made me! Come what may…

                    DORINE
Lovers never run out of things to say.
Leave, I tell you.

                    VALERE
        Starts to go, comes back.
            In short…

                    DORINE
                        Talk, talk, talk, talk!
Now get going, you two. And run, don't walk!

                Act III, scene 1
                Damis, Dorine

                    DAMIS
May lightening right this minute strike me down,
Let everyone call me the stupidest clown,
If anyone thinks they can stop me tonight
From settling things rashly with a big fight.

                    DORINE
There's no need to be as mad as you are.

Your father's done nothing but talk so far.
And from word to deed is a very long trip;
There's many a slip twixt the cup and the lip.

                    DAMIS
I've got to stop that rogue's conspiracy.
I'm going to tell him off! He'll hear from me!

                    DORINE
Calm down! See what your stepmother can do
To get around him and your father, too.
She has some influence on Tartuffe's mind;
Toward her he is always obliging and kind.
Maybe his heart has a weakness for her.
Pray God it's true! That would help us for sure.
She's just now sent for him, to sound him out
On this marriage you're so angry about.
She'll find out where he stands, then make him see
What terrible consequences there will be
If he helps Orgon to press this affair.
His valet told me he's busy in prayer
Now, but in a moment he'll come down here.
So please leave, would you? Don't try to interfere.

                    DAMIS
I can be present during this interview.

                    DORINE
No, they must be alone.

                    DAMIS
                    I promise you
I'll be quiet.

                    DORINE
                You're joking. I know your
Fits of anger. You'd spoil everything for sure.
Go on!

                    DAMIS
    I want to see! I won't get upset…

                    DORINE
You're so annoying! He's coming! Now get!

                Act III, scene 2

Tartuffe, Dorine, Laurent,
Damis (hiding)

TARTUFFE

Put away my hair shirt and whip, Laurent,
And pray for heaven to deliver us from taunt.
I'm off to the jail now, in desolation,
To help the poor prisoners' deprivation.

DORINE

What a bragging fake! What pretentious cheek!

TARTUFFE

What do you want?

DORINE
To say…

TARTUFFE
Mon Dieu! Don't speak
Until you take this handkerchief.

DORINE
What, me?

TARTUFFE
Takes out a handkerchief.
Cover that bosom which I must not see.
Souls can be wounded by objects like those;
That's why sinful and impure thoughts arose.

DORINE

Your soul is very weak against temptation
And very prone to fleshy stimulation.
I don't know what can turn on your fire,
For my part, I am slower to desire.
If I saw you naked, privates and all,
I wouldn't be tempted by something so small.

TARTUFFE

Temper your speech with modesty, my dear,
Or I shall go and leave you standing here.

DORINE

No, I'll leave you alone. I'm on my way.
But I have only a few words to say.
Madame Elmire, whom I believe you've met,

Would like to have a little tête-à-tête.

TARTUFFE

Alas! Quite gladly.

DORINE
How he softens down!
You just wait. I was right about that clown.

TARTUFFE

Will she come soon?

DORINE
That's her now, I believe.
Yes, here she is. And so, I'll take my leave.

Act III, scene 3
Elmire, Tartuffe, (Damis,
hiding)

TARTUFFE

May heaven in its grace preserve your body
And soul forever from all that is shoddy;
And bless your days, according to the love,
I humbly offer to the Lord above.

ELMIRE

I'm very obliged by a wish so pious,
But let's be seated and chat without bias.

TARTUFFE
Seated.
I trust your recent illness is all past?

ELMIRE
Seated.
Oh, yes, thank you. The fever did not last.

TARTUFFE

My small prayers were too unworthy, I feel
To have drawn from heaven the power to heal;
But your recovery has been the object of
Every prayer I've prayed to Heaven above.

ELMIRE

I don't deserve your excess of passion.

TARTUFFE
Your health is priceless, and in this fashion,
I'd give you my own, without temerity.

ELMIRE
You go too far with your Christian charity.
I fear your kindness leaves me your debtor.

TARTUFFE
I only wish I could serve you better.

ELMIRE
I've wanted to talk to you secretly,
And I'm glad that we have this privacy.

TARTUFFE
I'm glad, too. And I am very gratified
To find myself alone here by your side.
I've prayed to God for this opportunity,
But until now, it's always eluded me.

ELMIRE
I'd like a short talk, and I hope you'll be
Entirely open and honest with me.

*Damis, without being seen, opens the door of the
cabinet in which he is hiding in order to hear
the conversation.*

TARTUFFE
Indeed, my sole desire, all that I care –
To lay my soul before you perfectly bare.
I want you to know that the fuss I've made
About all of those visits that you've been paid,
Was not because of any hate I feel;
I was carried away by excess of zeal,
A pure desire…

ELMIRE
A pious aspiration.
Your only concern was my salvation.

TARTUFFE
Squeezes her fingers.
No doubt, Madame, and my fervor is such…

ELMIRE
You're squeezing too hard!

TARTUFFE
                    I just feel so much!
I would never hurt you because I care;
                    Puts his hand on her.
I'd rather…

ELMIRE
    What, pray, is your hand doing there?

TARTUFFE
Feeling your gown. It's so soft at the top.

ELMIRE
Oh, no, don't. I'm very ticklish. Please stop!

                    She pulls her chair away, and
                    he brings his closer to her.

TARTUFFE
        Feels her collar.
Mon Dieu! But this is such marvelous lace.
I love the way it compliments your face.
The workmanship's superb. It nothing lacks.

ELMIRE
Maybe, but let us get down to brass tacks.
My husband wants to give Mariane to you
And break his promise to her. Is that true?

TARTUFFE
He mentioned it, but I tell you in anguish,
That's not the happiness for which I languish.
It's elsewhere, Madame where I see the charms
That I long to hold tightly in my arms.

ELMIRE
You'd rather leave temporal things alone.

TARTUFFE
My breast does not contain a heart of stone.

ELMIRE
I think you love only the celestial
And not things of earth - low, base, and bestial.

TARTUFFE

To love eternal beauties far above
Does not mean I'm immune to earthly love.
Our senses may be easily awed
By those perfect works created by God.
This glory shows in some things by reflection
But you alone display its true perfection.
He has lavished such beauty on your face,
It dazzles the eyes and moves the heart apace.
I could not look at you, perfect creature,
And not admire the author of nature,
Feeling a love that makes my heart faint,
For you, the grand self-portrait he did paint.
At first I feared this secret affection
Was by the devil a clever deception.
And so I shunned you as a temptation,
An obstacle threatening my salvation.
But finally, oh gracious beauty, I knew
That this passion was not sinful, but true,
That I can reconcile it with propriety.
I surrender my heart without anxiety.
It is audacious, I know, on my part,
To dare to make this offering of my heart,
But my hopes all lie in your dear kindness,
And not in vain efforts of my weakness.
You are my hope, my peace, my salvation;
On you depends my joy - or desolation.
You'll decide my future, and I will be
Happy or unhappy, as you'd have me.

ELMIRE

A gallant speech, but rather surprising.
I'm puzzled to see these feelings arising.
You'd do better to think for a minute.
Look in your soul and see there what's in it.
You're so pious, so how is it you can…

TARTUFFE

I may be pious, but I'm still a man.
And when one sees your celestial splendor
The heart is captured and must surrender.
I know that such a speech from me seems queer,
But, Madame, there's no angel standing here.
And if you think that this brings me to shame,
It's your bewitching charms that are to blame.
The unfathomable sweetness of your glance

Crumbled my resistance far in advance,
You conquered all - fasting, prayer, and tears,
And I vowed to surrender all my fears.
My eyes, my sighs have shown how I adore;
My lips and my voice now say even more.
If you could allow your spirit to save
Me, and pity the pain of your poor slave;
If you would grant me consolation
And deign to comfort my humiliation,
Then nothing sweet marvel, could be as true
As the constant devotion I'll have for you.
Your honor won't be placed in jeopardy,
And you won't run a single risk with me.
Those court gallants on whom the ladies dote
Are far too noisy and too prone to gloat.
When they succeed in love, the world soon knows it;
When a favor's granted, they soon disclose it.
Men like me, however, are much more discreet.
We keep secrets. Let your trust be complete.
I take a lot of care with my good name;
You can trust that with yours I'll do the same.
If you accept, what you'll get is, Elmire,
Love without scandal, pleasure without fear.

                    ELMIRE
I've listened to your fancy speeches, and
What you are proposing, I understand.
Aren't you afraid of the possibility
I'll tell my husband of your love for me?
Your romantic ardor, if he ever knew,
Might undermine his affection for you.

                    TARTUFFE
I know you are gracious and benign
And will pardon this audacity of mine;
That you will excuse my violent fancies
As the workings of my masculine frailties.
Looking in your mirror, please keep in mind,
A man is flesh and blood, and I'm not blind.

                    ELMIRE
Another woman might not do this,
But here's how I'm going to see us through this.
I won't tell my husband about what I've learned
If you promise me one thing in return.
And that's to argue, as hard as you can
For the marriage of Valere and Mariane.

And never again try to make some gain
Out of someone else's misery and pain,
And…

Act III, scene 4
Elmire, Damis, Tartuffe

DAMIS

    No, Madame, no. This must be revealed.
I heard everything where I was concealed.
Heaven's goodness must have hid me there to
Demolish the pride of that traitor who
Has been harming us. Now, at last, vengeance
Is mine. His hypocrisy and insolence
Will be exposed. I will wise up my Dad
About this would be lover and cad.

ELMIRE

No, Damis. It's enough if he repents
And vows to live a life of better sense.
I've promised silence, and I won't break my trust;
It's not in my nature to make a big fuss.
A wife can laugh off the nonsense she hears
Without ever alarming her husband's ears.

DAMIS

You have your reasons for acting as you do,
And for what I'm doing, I have reasons, too.
It would be ludicrous to spare him now.
I've held my temper too long, seeing how
That sanctimonious slob has brought disarray
Into this family's life every day.
Too long that cheat has run father's affairs
Screwing up my love-life, and poor Valere's.
But no more. I must expose his treachery,
And now heaven gives me the opportunity.
I'm deeply indebted to it for this,
'Cause this opportunity is too good to miss.

ELMIRE

Damis…

DAMIS

    No! I'm right. I know. Please don't insist;
I've never been near as happy as this.
And no matter what you say, I will not
Give up the sweet revenge I've finally got.
It's time we settled all this, anyhow,
And here comes my opportunity now!

Act III, scene 5
Orgon, Elmire, Damis,
Tartuffe

DAMIS

Father, I'm glad you're here. I have a tale
I'm sure will take the wind out of your sail.
You've been paid back, with interest, I fear
For all that you have done for this guy here.
He's shown the true values by which he is led;
He wants to dishonor your marriage bed.
He tried to seduce your wife, and I heard
His vows of guilty passion, every word.
Madame, on account of her fortitude,
Was not gonna tell you of his plan so lewd.
But there's a thirst for revenge in my heart,
And I will not play a forgiving part.

ELMIRE

And I think a husband should not be put out
By nonsense that comes from the mouth of a lout.
I assure you my honor's not in danger;
I know how to shield myself from a stranger.
Those are my feelings, and I wish, Damis
That you'd listened to me and held your peace.
                    Exits.
                    Act III, scene 6
                    Orgon, Damis, Tartuffe

ORGON

What I have just heard, oh God! Is it true?

TARTUFFE

Yes, brother, I'm guilty, and evil, too.
Miserable, wicked, filled with sin,
The greatest scoundrel there's ever been.
Each minute of my life is covered with grime;
I'm merely a mass of dirt, dung, and crime.
And I see that heaven, to castigate me
Takes this occasion to humiliate me.
Charge me with any crime that you can name,
I won't defend myself, such is my shame.
Believe what you are told, and drive Tartuffe
Like a criminal from under your roof.
No matter whatever shame lies in store
For me, I know that I deserve much more.

ORGON
To Damis.
Ah, you wretched traitor! How dare you try
To stain his purity with that foul lie?

DAMIS
What? How are you taken in by that dreck?
Didn't you…

ORGON
Shut up, you pain in the neck!

TARTUFFE

No! Let him speak, you're wrong to accuse him;
Between us, you'd do better to choose him.
How do you know what I might do, where I'd go?
Do you trust me because of my outward show?
No, don't be deceived by my appearance
Deep down inside, I'm much worse than you sense.
Everyone looks at me like I'm a hero,
But the real truth is that I'm worth zero.
       To Damis.
Yes, my son, call me any name in the book –
Villain, betrayer, murderer, and crook.
Go ahead and call me anything worse
I'll take all of it; I deserve the curse.
I'll suffer this disgrace - just let me kneel here -
A just punishment for all that I feel here.

ORGON
Brother, this is too much.
      To Damis.
          Is your heart breaking,
Traitor?

DAMIS
What? Can't you see that he's faking?

ORGON
Shut up, scoundrel.
      To Tartuffe.
        Up, my brother, please rise.
      To Damis.
Wretch!

DAMIS
He can...

ORGON
Shut up!

DAMIS
I can't believe my eyes!

ORGON
Just say one more word and I'll break your arm.

TARTUFFE
Brother, in the name of God, please be calm!
I would rather suffer the deepest pain
Than have him receive one scratch in my name.

ORGON
To Damis.
Ingrate!

TARTUFFE
If I must, I'll get down on my knees
And beg you to forgive him.

ORGON
*Gets on his knees, embraces
Tartuffe.*
Alas! Please!
To Damis.
Dog! Look at his goodness.

DAMIS
So...

ORGON
Peace!

DAMIS
But...

ORGON
Quiet!
I know why you attack him. Don't deny it.
I see clearly now how you all hate him,
And you've formed a conspiracy to bait him.
In your impudence, there's no trick too quaint

To try and separate me from this saint.
But it won't work. Try to drive him away,
I'll work that much harder to make him stay.
I'll hasten his marriage to Mariane,
And confound this family the best way I can.

DAMIS
And you'll force this marriage just out of spite?

ORGON
Yes, and to get you, I'll do it tonight.
I'll defy you all. You've got to learn faster
How to obey me and who is the master.
Apologize, rascal, for what you said;
Get down on your knees, and lower your head.

DAMIS
I'm supposed to apologize to that bore?…

ORGON
You dare to refuse, then insult him some more?
Give me a stick! A stick!
            To Tartuffe.
                    Don't hold me back.
            To Damis.
Get out of my house. Now. Don't stop to pack.
The sight of your face here will make me sick.

DAMIS
All right, I'll go, but…

ORGON
                Get out of here, quick!
I disinherit you, and what is worse,
What I will give you, scoundrel, is my curse.

            Act III, scene 7
            Orgon, Tartuffe

ORGON
Such profane blasphemy he said to you.

TARTUFFE
Father, forgive them, they know not what they do.
            TO ORGON.
This pain that I feel is like no other.
To be slandered like that in front of my brother.

ORGON

Alas.

TARTUFFE
          The mere thought of such ingratitude
Makes my soul suffer a torture so rude…
My broken heart is filled with horror. I
Can't speak, and I know that I shall die.

ORGON
              In tears, he runs to the door
              through which he has just driven
              out his son.
Scoundrel! I spared you, but why did I not
Grab you and knock you down, right on the spot?
                    To Tartuffe.
Compose yourself, brother; don't be distressed.

TARTUFFE
From these dreadful fights I can find no rest.
I see how I upset things. I believe
That the best thing for me to do is leave.

ORGON
What? Are you serious?

TARTUFFE
                    They all can't abide me.
It drives them crazy to see you beside me.

ORGON
I don't listen to them. I believe in you.

TARTUFFE
But their accusations will continue.
And these same stories, which now you reject,
You might one day, brother, be forced to accept.

ORGON
No, brother, never.

TARTUFFE
              But brother, a wife
Can change a husband's mind and run his life.

ORGON

No, no.

TARTUFFE

    If I leave, then they can't fault me,
They'll have no more reason to assault me.

ORGON

No. You will stay, not leave. I won't hear it.

TARTUFFE

All right, I'll stay - to mortify my spirit.
Still, if you wanted…

ORGON

    Oh!

TARTUFFE

    Let it be so.
I think there's something I must do, you know.
Honor is delicate, and friendship means
That I should protect you from all these scenes.
I'll avoid you wife; you won't see me near her…

ORGON

No, to spite them, you'll always be near her.
To enrage the world is my greatest delight
And I want you seen with her day and night.
That's not all. To defy them through and through,
I want to have no other heir but you.
And, so that my devotion may be shown,
I'll give to you everything that I own.
A good, dear friend, my son-in-law for life,
Means more to me than family, son, or wife.
Won't you accept from me all that I've given?

TARTUFFE

God's will be done, on earth as 'tis in heaven.

ORGON

The poor fellow! Let's get the deed drawn up right.
And from it may the jealous burst with spite.

End of Act III

INTERMISSION

ACT IV, scene 1
Cleante, Tartuffe, Laurent

CLEANTE

Everyone's talking about it. This story,
Believe me, adds little to your glory.
And it's quite fortunate that I found you
To give my opinion in a word or two.
I won't try to say who's wrong or who's right,
But just look at things in the very worst light.
Let us suppose that Damis is to blame
But that, just the same, it's you they defame.
Shouldn't a Christian pardon the offense
And thus extinguish his rage for vengeance?
Because of your fight, will you allow this child,
The son by his father to be exiled?
I tell you frankly, you've been much too hard,
Everyone's scandalized by it - no holds barred.
And if you believe me, you would make peace.
Don't carry things to extremes with poor Damis.
Sacrifice your anger to God above,
And let the son regain his father's love.

TARTUFFE

Alas, I would love to, with all my heart.
I hold no bitterness for him on my part.
I forgive him everything, as I should,
And with my soul would love to do him good.
But Heaven, I fear offers no reprieve;
If he comes back here, then I'll have to leave.
After his actions, which were out of place,
We can't associate without disgrace.
God knows what everyone's first thoughts would be—
Of sheer calculation they'd accuse me.
They'd say that because of the guilt I feel,
I feign for my accuser a loving zeal.
That I'd try out of fear and self-interest,
To force his silence and let matters rest.

CLEANTE

You want to make it seem that you've been wronged,
But all your reasoning is much too prolonged.
Why do you take on heaven's interests?
Does God need us to know which punishment's best?
Let God take care of his own vengeances.
We've been ordered to forgive offenses.
And whether men speak of you well or ill,

It doesn't matter. Just follow God's will.
What? Should the fear of being misunderstood
Prevent you from doing what's truly good?
No, let us do what Heaven has ordered
And by nothing else let our minds be tortured.

TARTUFFE
My heart forgives him, as I have told you,
And that is what God commands me to do.
But nothing in the Bible says that I should
Pretend that his smears are actually good.

CLEANTE
Then, Monsieur, does it order you rather
To listen to the whim of his father –
To accept the gift of this entire home
Which you've no right to call your own?

TARTUFFE
Anyone who knows me well is, I'm sure,
Quite aware that my motives are all pure.
The wealth of this earth does not dazzle me;
Its tawdry luster does not frazzle me.
And if I have resolved myself to take
The gift that Orgon insisted to make,
It's only, to tell the truth, because I fear
That it might fall into wicked hands here.
These riches could buy things not very nice,
Pay for a life of crime, sin, sleaze, and vice.
They wouldn't use this treasure as I would,
For Heaven's glory, and my neighbor's good.

CLEANTE
Your fears, Monsieur, are rather sophistical,
If not, indeed, a little egotistical.
Leave Damis the estate. It is his wealth.
He's a big boy and can look after himself.
I am surprised that you could have taken
Orgon's donations without being shaken.
Is there some holy maxim that declares
It's okay to rob from legitimate heirs?
And if the Lord spoke to you, saying, "My man,
You can't live with Damis, you must understand,"
Wouldn't it be best, in a manner discreet,
To leave this place in an honest retreat,
Rather than to know that, because of you
The good son is disowned and banished, too?

Believe me, Monsieur, your integrity
Would not seem…

TARTUFFE
It is, Monsieur, half past three.
I've pious devotions at this time of day,
And you will excuse me if I don't stay.
Exits.

CLEANTE
Alone.
Damn.

Act IV, scene 2
*Elmire, Mariane, Cleante,
Dorine*

DORINE
To Cleante.
Stay, help us, please. This is such a shame.
Mariane is suffering a terrible pain.
Her father's planned the wedding tonight. There
Is no hope for her. She's plunged in despair.
He's coming. Let's all work together now,
To try and make him change his mind somehow
About this before we're ruined forever.

Act IV, scene 3
*Orgon, Elmire, Mariane,
Cleante, Dorine*

ORGON
Ah! I'm glad to find you all together.
To Mariane.
I've a contract which assures your happiness,
And you know already what I mean by this.

MARIANE
On her knees.
Father, by heaven, which knows how I grieve,
By everything that can move your heart, please
Waive some of your fatherly rights, I pray,
And in this do not force me to obey.
And, alas, this, my life which you gave me,
Don't take its happiness and thus enslave me.
If you must deny me my hope and prayer
Of marrying the man I love, Valere,

At least, be kind; on my knees I implore,
Don't make me marry a man I abhor.
And don't drive me to the point of despair
By using your power to force this affair.

ORGON
Touched.
No human weakness, now. Be firm my heart.

MARIANE
I don't mind the feelings for him on your part.
Give him all your wealth, and shout it out loud!
And if he wants more, take mine, I'm not proud.
Take all my money, whatever you feel,
But don't include me as part of the deal.
Let me retreat to a convent, I pray
And live my life there, sad day after day.

ORGON
A convent! What a daughter! Everyone
When her love is once crossed must be a nun!
Get up! The more you think you cannot bear it,
The greater happiness in heaven you'll merit.
Marry Tartuffe and mortify your senses.
That's enough of your female defenses.

DORINE
But what…

ORGON
    Shut up, you! Speak when you're spoken to.
I don't want another word out of you.

CLEANTE
If I may, I'll offer you some advice…

ORGON
Brother, your advice is always quite nice,
Cogent, reasonable, no doubt about it,
But I think I'll manage just fine without it.

ELMIRE
Seeing what I see, words totally fail
Me. And your blindness is beyond the pale.
You must be quite bewitched by him, I'd say,
To doubt us about what happened today.

ORGON

I beg to differ. I know the facts here.
You've always favored my stupid son, dear.
You know you were afraid to disavow
The scheme he tried to put over just now.
But you underplayed your part; you were too calm,
You should have shown more anger, more alarm.

ELMIRE

If someone tells me he loves me wrongly,
Must my honor take offense so strongly>
I'd rather laugh at those propositions,
And not make a scene under such conditions.
I don't wave my honor like a flag,
Or scratch and hiss like some old hag.
Heaven preserve me from virtue like that.
I want to be decent, not an alley cat.
I'm convinced that a cool and simple "no"
Will tell unwelcome lovers where to go.

ORGON

I know all the facts, and I will not change.

ELMIRE

Your weakness amazes me, it's quite strange.
But I'm just wondering what you would do
If you could see that what we say is true.

ORGON

See it?

ELMIRE

        Yes.

ORGON

            Nonsense.

ELMIRE

                Try this on for size:
I can make you see it with your own eyes.

ORGON

Fairy tales.

ELMIRE

        Oh, what a man! Listen, you must.
I'm not asking you to take it on trust.

Suppose that we find you someplace to hide
Where you can see all that happens inside.
What would you say, seeing your god fall?

ORGON

In that case I'd say…I'd say nothing at all.
It can't be true.

ELMIRE

You've been deceived too long,
And you've got to stop thinking that I'm wrong.
For my satisfaction, then, and your proof
I'm going to make you witness the truth.

ORGON

All right, I'll do it. Let's have your little show.
I guess I'll find out what I'm supposed to know.

ELMIRE
To Dorine.
Send him here to me.

DORINE

You know that he's slick.
He's going to be a hard one to trick.

ELMIRE

No. One is easily fooled by that which one
Loves, and self-love leads to self-deception.
Go get him.
To Cleante and Mariane.
Please leave us alone for a bit.

Act IV, scene 4
Elmire, Orgon

ELMIRE

Come here to this table and get under it.

ORGON

What?

ELMIRE

You've got to be totally out of sight.

ORGON

Why under there?

ELMIRE
Oh my God, please don't fight.
I have my plan, you'll judge this affair.
Get down now, I tell you, and when you're there,
Be careful you don't give yourself away.

ORGON
I said I'd do it, so this game I'll play.
I'll be patient and see the whole thing through.

ELMIRE
And one fine day you'll thank me if you do.
                    *To her husband, who is now under
                    the table.*
I'm going to be acting rather strange,
And I do not want you getting deranged.
Whatever I say, it must be understood
It's to convince you, as I said I would.
Since I've been forced into this, I will use
Sweet words of love to unmask his ruse,
Awaken his passion and lewd desires,
And fan the flames of his amorous fires.
Since this is for you, and to bring him to harm,
I'll pretend to be seduced by his charm.
I'll stop when you think that this should be through;
Things will go just as far as you want them to.
Once you are convinced that he is at fault,
It's up to you to call things to a halt.
This is all about you, so what you say will
Be…He's coming. Keep hidden and be still.

                    Act IV, scene 5
                    *Tartuffe, Elmire, Orgon
                    (under the table)*

TARTUFFE
I was told to come down and speak with you.

ELMIRE
Yes, I've got something to say *entre nous*.
But first close that door. And it would be wise
To look around there, for fear of surprise.
                    *Tartuffe closes the door and comes
                    back.*
We certainly don't want a repetition
Of what happened last time in the position.
I was so surprised, and totally manic;

Damis for you put me in a panic.
And you saw how I tried to calm him down,
But he's such a volatile little clown.
So, in my confusion, I lost my head
And didn't think to deny the things he said.
But even that, thank God, worked out very well,
And things are much safer now, I can tell.
The storm's passed, thanks to your esteemed position,
And my husband hasn't the least suspicion.
But to spite the suspicious, however,
He wants us always to be together.
And that's how I can, without fear of blame
Be locked in here with you, my heart aflame,
And reveal that I have allowed you to touch
Me deeply…But perhaps I've said too much.

                    TARTUFFE
You're quite difficult, Madame, to discern;
You spoke quite differently on the last turn.

                    ELMIRE
Ah, if that upset you, that just goes to show
About a woman's heart how little you know.
You can't tell what we really want to say
When we protest in such a feeble way.
No matter how powerful is our flame,
We can never admit it without shame.
For honor, we say no, but can't you guess
That what we really mean is to whisper "yes."
I'm afraid I'm speaking rather freely,
Without much regard for my modesty,
But, tell me, since I've dared to say all that,
Would I have struggled to hold Damis back,
And would I have, so calmly on my part,
Listened so long to the offer of your heart,
And would I have reacted in such a fashion
If I had not been pleased by your passion?
And when I tried to force you not to go through
With the marriage plans my husband has for you,
To you what should my urgent prayer suggest,
If not my deep and personal interest?
My fear, dear Tartuffe, is if you got her,
I'd then have to share you with my daughter.

                    TARTUFFE
It is no doubt, Madame, an extreme bliss
When I hear you speak to me words like this.

Their honey inundates me completely,
Its undreamed of sweetness stroking so sweetly.
Pleasing you is the greatest joy I know of;
My heart finds its happiness in your love.
But this heart asks you now the liberty
To dare to question its felicity.
These words could be a scheme, part of a plan
To make me break off my marriage with Mariane.
I mean, speaking candidly, as I must,
Mere sweet words alone cannot win my trust,
Until you go beyond mere talk to deeds,
And give me a taste of what my heart needs,
And until you fill my soul and my arms
With your kindness and those bewitching charms.

ELMIRE
Coughs, to warn her husband.
Well, what's your hurry? Here we are at last,
Don't push our love to its climax so fast.
I forced myself to make that fond admission,
But would you add another condition—
That you will not be satisfied unless
At once I grant my utmost tenderness?

TARTUFFE
The promise of joy cures not the fever;
We need the real thing to be a believer.
I'm unworthy - I've not the capacity
To be happy - I've too much audacity.
I will believe nothing you can name
Until realities convince my flame.

ELMIRE
My, but your love is the tyrannical kind,
That puts me in a troubled state of mind.
I'm quite overwhelmed, and breathing harder,
Is there no denying your violent ardor?
Come now, you can't want to run me to death
And not give me a chance to catch my breath!

TARTUFFE
But if you sincerely love your Tartuffe,
Why do you refuse to give me some proof?

ELMIRE
If I consented, I would without a doubt
Offend Heaven, which you always talk about.

TARTUFFE

Heaven? If that's all that's holding you back,
I know how to get you back on track.
There's no need to restrain your heart's desire.

ELMIRE

But they scare us so with tales of hellfire.

TARTUFFE[1]

Forget that fear. Be one of my pupils.
I know the art of removing scruples.
There're some pleasures it's true that Heaven denies,
But Heaven's not averse to compromise.
There is a new science now that succeeds
In stretching consciences to meet one's needs.
You can rectify the evil of a sin
With the purity of a good intention.
All these secrets I can teach you, Elmire,
If you'll trust me and follow without fear.
Satisfy my desires, and you'll be fine.
If there's any sin, we'll just say it's mine.
            Elmire coughs more loudly
You've a bad cough.

ELMIRE
            Yes, I can't seem to stop.

TARTUFFE

How about a little licorice cough drop?

ELMIRE

It's a persistent cold, and I don't see how
All the licorice in the world can help me now.

TARTUFFE

How aggravating.

ELMIRE
            More than I can say.

TARTUFFE

To destroy a scruple, think of it this way -
The secret is ours - that's as far as it goes;
There is no sin unless someone else knows.

---

[1] Moliere adds a footnote to this speech, reminding us that "It is a scoundrel speaking."

Scandal is evil and creates the fall;
To sin in secret is not sinning at all.

ELMIRE
Coughs again and pounds the table.
I see now I have to lay down my arms,
And let you enjoy all of my charms.
To make you happy and to win your trust,
Since nothing else will do, I guess I must.
I wish you were not so demanding, though,
You've pushed me farther than I want to go.
But since no one is listening to what I say,
My actions will have to carry the day.
And since you require absolute conviction,
I must decide to give satisfaction.
If I am wrong, and if I sin through it,
Too bad for the man who made me do it.
And I'm not to blame, most assuredly.

TARTUFFE
I'll take the full responsibility.

ELMIRE
But open the door first, please, and take a glance
To see if my husband's there, by any chance.

TARTUFFE
Why worry about precautions like those?
He is the type you can lead by the nose.
He could be observing all that we do,
And, even then, he still wouldn't have a clue.

ELMIRE
Just the same, I would feel much more secure
If you'd take a look 'round, just to be sure.

Act IV, scene 6
Orgon, Elmire

ORGON
Coming out from under the table.
Now that is an abominable man!
I'm astounded! I don't see how I can…

ELMIRE
What? Coming out so soon? That's crazy, my pet.
Get back under there! Nothing's happened yet.

Wait until the end, so you can make sure
You won't have to trust to mere conjecture.

                    ORGON
Nothing more evil ever came from Hell!

                    ELMIRE
Ah, you can't believe the stories they tell.
Just take your time - perhaps you're mistaken.
Don't let your faith be so easily shaken.
                    Puts her husband behind her as
                    Tartuffe re-enters.

                    Act IV, scene 7
                    Tartuffe, Elmire, Orgon,
                    Laurent

                    TARTUFFE
          Without seeing Orgon.
Everything conspires in our favor, my dear.
I took a look around, and the coast is clear.
No one's there, so now I may at last…

                    ORGON
          Intercepts him.
Just a minute, loverboy, not so fast!
You must not let your passions run so free.
Ha! You holy man, you thought you'd fool me.
You surely let temptation rule your life!
Marry my daughter and seduce my wife!
I always doubted what I should have known,
But I kept hoping you would change your tone.
But now I have seen enough and I've heard
Enough. I don't need to hear another word.

                    ELMIRE
I'm sorry I had to treat you this way,
But that was the part I was forced to play.

                    TARTUFFE
What? Can you believe…

                    ORGON
              That's enough out of you.
Get out of this house without further ado.

TARTUFFE

How I meant it...

ORGON

I don't care to know how.
Get out of this house, and I mean now.

TARTUFFE

No. You've got to leave. Try that on for size.
This house belongs to me, don't you realize?
In no time at all you'll be sorry to see
That you ever tried to pick a fight with me.
You're in a bad position to throw insults,
I've got the power to show you results.
I'll avenge Heaven, and make you repent
That you ever dared ask me to relent.

Act IV, scene 8
Elmire, Orgon

ELMIRE

What in the world did he mean by what he said?

ORGON

This is no laughing matter, dear. We're dead.

ELMIRE

What's wrong?

ORGON

I'm afraid I gave it short shrift -
I am worried about that deed of gift.

ELMIRE

A deed of gift?

ORGON

Yes, it's been signed already.
But there's something else making me unsteady.

ELMIRE

What?

ORGON

Wait - before continuing our talks,
Let's go upstairs and look for a strongbox.

Act V, scene 1
Orgon, Cleante

CLEANTE
Where're you rushing to?

ORGON
I'm not sure, brother!

CLEANTE
We should figure out something or other.
It looks like things have taken a bad turn.

ORGON
That strongbox is my primary concern.
It above all else drives me to despair.

CLEANTE
This strongbox then's an important affair?

ORGON
My poor friend Argas, he gave it me
Himself, and with the utmost secrecy.
When he was exiled, he came first to me,
Saying that his life and all his property
Depended on the papers left in there.

CLEANTE
To let Tartuffe have them - how could you dare?

ORGON
By his persuasion, he got me to agree
To put the strongbox in his custody.
So if they came to investigate,
I could play dumb and prevaricate,
And swear I did not have it, and so,
Tell a lie, but that way no one would know.

CLEANTE
It seems to me that your prospects look dim;
That deed of gift, your confidence in him,
Were both, speaking frankly, not politely,
Bad steps on your part taken rather lightly.
With these two weapons, I fear he's got you
Right where he wants you now. You forgot you
Were grappling with a man of many schemes.
You never should have pushed him to extremes.

ORGON

I took him in, a penniless beggar.
That's it! I renounce pious men forever!

CLEANTE

There you go again - with exasperation.
You're never content with moderation.
You never find the reasonable pathway;
On the extremes, you never go halfway.
Be more cautious in lending your esteem,
And carefully avoid any extreme.

Act V, scene 2
Damis, Orgon, Cleante

DAMIS

What? Dad, that scoundrel is bullying you,
Forgetting all your kindness? Is that true?
With his cowardly pride he now threatens
To use your gifts against you as weapons?

ORGON

Yes, my son. It's true. I am close to tears.

DAMIS

Just let me at him; I'll cut off his ears.
Against his insolence we must not waver.
Of getting rid of him, I'll do the favor.
Just let me strike him down and you'll be freed.

CLEANTE

Now there's a young man's solution, indeed.
Calm down, please, this raging virility.
Our progressive age needs less hostility.
We must move beyond our violent history.

Act V, scene 3
Madame Pernelle, Flipote,
Orgon, Elmire, Cleante,
Mariane, Damis, Dorine

MME. PERNELLE

What's going on? What is this mystery?

ORGON

There are strange things I've seen with my own eyes!

A reward for my kindness, and a surprise.
I take in and save a man from misery,
And he becomes like a brother to me.
Every day my kindness he is shown,
I gave him my daughter and all I own;
And now, he'll drive me out, a ruined man,
And leave me in the gutter, where he began.

DORINE
The poor fellow!

MME. PERNELLE
No, son. I never had
The slightest idea he could be that bad.

ORGON
What?

MME. PERNELLE
People always envy a righteous man.

ORGON
Mother, make yourself clearer, if you can.

MME. PERNELLE
In this strange place, you all think he's a louse.
I know everyone hates him in this house.

ORGON
What does that hate have to do with his crimes?

MME. PERNELLE
When you were a boy, I told you many times
"Virtue in this world is hated forever.
The envious will die, but envy never."

ORGON
Maybe, but I don't see how it applies.

MME. PERNELLE
They've turned you against him with crafty lies.

ORGON
I tell you I saw that philanderer.

MME. PERNELLE
Whoever said that is a slanderer.

ORGON

Mother, I will lose my temper. I've told
You, I saw him commit this crime so bold.

MME. PERNELLE

Malicious tongues will their venom spread
And nothing will stop them before they're dead.

ORGON

This is nonsense. Get it through your thick skull,
I saw it, I tell you, saw; are you dull?
Saw, do you understand? Must I shout it
Ninety times before you'll cease to doubt it?

MME. PERNELLE

Appearance are deceiving, mercy me!
We must not always judge by what we see.

ORGON

I'm going mad.

MME. PERNELLE

                Beware of false suspicions.
Good may seem bad under some conditions.

ORGON

And when he tries to take to bed my wife,
Should I call this charity?

MME. PERNELLE

                            In this life,
We should give men the benefit of the doubt.
You could have waited to see how it turned out.

ORGON

Oh my God! How in the hell could I be
More sure? Did you want me to wait to see
Them…Oh, my God, you're making this harder.

MME. PERNELLE

His soul is filled with such holy ardor,
I believe in him, I do. You can't shake me.
I won't change my mind, and you can't make me.

ORGON

Ah! If you weren't my mother, I don't know
What I'd do, you infuriate me so.

DORINE
To Orgon.
The tables are turned. It's poetic justice.
She won't trust you just as you wouldn't trust us.

CLEANTE
We're wasting time with this stupid baloney;
We must find a way to stop this phony.
His threats weren't empty, or made in sport.

DAMIS
Do you think he'll try to take us to court?

ELMIRE
Well, I don't think that that is possible.
His ingratitude is all too visible.

CLEANTE
Don't be too sure. He has secret ways, no doubt
With which he might well twist the truth about.

ELMIRE
If I had have known what cards he held in hand,
I'd have thought twice about the trick I planned,
And…

ORGON
To Dorine, seeing Monsieur Loyal
Who is that man? I'm in a fine state
For visitors. Go find out. This is just great.

Act V, scene 4
*Orgon, Madame Pernelle,
Flipote, Elmire, Mariane,
Cleante, Damis, Dorine,
Monsieur Loyal*

M. LOYAL
To Dorine.
Good day, my dear sister. Please let me see
The master of the house.

DORINE
He has company,
And really cannot see anyone now.

M. LOYAL

I hate to intrude, but why I've come and how
Are particulars that I know won't displease.
In fact, I'm sure they will put him at ease.

DORINE

What is your name?

M. LOYAL

        Just tell him, if you would,
I come from Monsieur Tartuffe, for his own good.

DORINE

To Orgon.

He is a messenger, and quite soft-spoken,
From our Tartuffe. He says he brings a token
Of his regard.

CLEANTE

        You had just better see
Who this man is and what his news could be.

ORGON

Perhaps he'll suggest some kind of agreement.
What'll I do, give him what kind of treatment?

CLEANTE

Don't let your anger carry you away.
And if he talks peace, let him have his say.

M. LOYAL

Good health, sire, may heaven confound your enemies,
And may joy abound, as much as you please.

ORGON

To Cleante.

That sweet greeting shows my judgment was wise;
He's here to offer a compromise.

M. LOYAL

Your household has always been dear to me.
I was your father's servant here, you see.

ORGON

Sir, I beg your pardon, but to my shame,
I must admit I can't recall your name.

M. LOYAL

I'm from Normandy, and Loyal's the name,
And as you can see, bailiff is my game.
For forty years I have served, thanks to God,
With honor and happiness having this job.
And I've come to you, sire, if you'll permit
To summon you with this judicial writ.

ORGON

What? You are here to…

M. LOYAL
                    Monsieur, please don't shout.
It's nothing but a summons to move out.
You, your family, the whole household must go
So that someone else can move in. Just so
There's no unwanted delay, give the keys…

ORGON

Me? Leave this house?

M. LOYAL
                    Why, yes, Sire, if you
please.
This house now belongs to good Monsieur Tartuffe,
And here is all you need by way of proof.
From now on, he's master of this estate
By virtue of this deed with today's date.
It's drawn in good form, and perfectly phrased.

DAMIS

Your impudence is great, and I'm amazed.

M. LOYAL

Young man, my business here is not with you,
But with your father. Remove yourself from view.

ORGON

But…

M. LOYAL

    I know you won't fight me for a million francs,
And for that you'll earn my respect and thanks.
I know you won't make trouble or interfere
With the execution of my duties here.

DAMIS

You think you're so special with that big stick;
What if I hit you with it and make you sick!

M. LOYAL

To Orgon.

Sire, please make your son leave or be quiet;
If I report him as causing a riot,
We'd then be forced to throw the book at him.

DORINE

Aside.

He should be Dis<u>loyal</u> by the look of him.

M. LOYAL

I have a great respect for honesty,
And I agreed to serve this writ, you see,
Just to ensure that things were nicely done,
And to keep them from assigning anyone
Else, who might not share my admiration,
And would proceed with less consideration.

ORGON

And where, my friend, can you find a worse crime
Than evicting a man?

M. LOYAL

I'm giving you time.

Stay until tomorrow as your reprieve,
And only then will I force you to leave.
I will just stay here tonight to sleep, then,
Upsetting nothing with ten of my men.
Just for form's sake, as I told you before,
You must give me the keys to your front door.
My men, I promise, won't interfere with you,
They will just sort of, well, be here with you.
But early tomorrow, and quickly, too,
You must leave this house and take nothing with you.
I'm the nicest man in the world, that's true,
And since I've been so very good to you,
And kindness, we know, always comes back double;
I ask that you not give me any trouble.

ORGON

Aside.

To reward this fool for all that he said
I'd like to smack him once upside the head.

CLEANTE
Quietly, to Orgon.
Careful. Don't spoil things.

DAMIS
                              My fist is itching.
Just let me slug him and stop his bitching.

DORINE
Monsieur Loyal, my, but you've got a nice back;
And how I'd love to give it a good whack.

M. LOYAL
Take care. Women are not above the law.
You could go to jail with your flapping jaw.

CLEANTE
Let's have no more of this, sir. Pray you, cease.
Just serve your paper and leave us in peace.

M. LOYAL
Au revoir! It's been a joy on my part.

ORGON
I'll tell you what - I don't give a good fart!

Act V, scene 5
Orgon, Madame Pernelle,
Flipote, Elmire, Cleante,
Mariane, Damis, Dorine

ORGON
Well, you see, I was right about Tartuffe,
Mother. This summons should give you clear proof.
You see how long his treachery has lasted?

MME. PERNELLE
I don't know what to say. I'm flabbergasted.

DORINE
But you're doing wrong to blame him, really.
He's thinking of you. I see that clearly.
He's consumed with love for all of mankind,
And knowing that wealth can corrupt and blind,
He robbed you to remove sin's temptation,
And thus give a clear road to salvation.

ORGON

Shut up. That's what I always have to say.

CLEANTE

We'd better decide what to do right away.

ELMIRE

Go tell the world of his audacity.
The contract's voided by his mendacity.
We must arouse the public opinion,
And expose the treachery of this minion.

                    Act V, scene 6
                    *Valere, Orgon, Madame
                    Pernelle, Flipote, Elmire,
                    Cleante, Mariane, Damis,
                    Dorine*

VALERE

          Enters.
I am sorry to bring you bad news, sir.
But I must, for you are in great danger.
Things have got worse, there's to be no reprieve,
And for your own safety, you must now leave.
The scoundrel who swindled you in everything
Denounced you an hour ago to the King;
And as supporting evidence, the fox
Brought out a certain renegade's strongbox,
Which he says you've hidden illegally,
Ignoring a loyal subject's duty.
My information is lacking in detail,
But there's a warrant out to take you to jail.
They've even deputized Tartuffe, I fear,
To escort the police officer here.

ORGON

That man is a most evil animal.

VALERE

The slightest delay now would be fatal.
My carriage is waiting to take you away
With a thousand francs to help on your way.
Let's waste no time. We'll find a safer site.
I'll stay with you till the end of your flight.

ORGON

Alas! I only wish I could show you
My gratitude for all that I owe you.
May Heaven some day give the opportunity
To thank you for your generosity.
Adieu; be careful, all…

CLEANTE

You're moving too slow!
We'll take care of everything, so you just go!

Act V, scene 7
Officer, Tartuffe, Laurent,
Madame Pernelle, Flipote,
Orgon, Elmire, Cleante,
Mariane, Valere, Damis,
Dorine

TARTUFFE

Gently, monsieur, gently. Why go so fast?
Where are you going? Your freedom is past.
We hereby arrest you in the King's name.

ORGON

Traitor, so you've brought me to this last shame.
This is the stroke, scoundrel, that's brought me down.
Of all your villainies, this wears the crown.

TARTUFFE

Your insults do not aggravate me, love.
I've been taught patience by Heaven above.

CLEANTE

That's great moderation, I must admit.

DAMIS

Such insolence! I can't get over it.

TARTUFFE

You cannot move me with your mockery.
Doing my duty means everything to me.

MARIANE

How are you honorable in any way?
And where is the glory in what you say?

                    TARTUFFE
Mademoiselle, I find glory in everything,
When I'm doing the duty of the King.

                    ELMIRE
Impostor!

                    DORINE
        He takes everything we esteem
And twists it all around to serve his scheme.

                    TARTUFFE
            To the Officer.
Deliver me, please, from this bleeding heart.
You have your orders, so now play your part.

                    OFFICER
Yes, I've been waiting too long to do it,
And it's only right that you urge me to it.
So here's the order - kindly follow me
To the prison that's your new home-to-be.

                    TARTUFFE
Who, I, sir?

                    OFFICER
            Yes, you.

                    TARTUFFE
                But why to prison?

                    OFFICER
It's not to you I owe an explanation.

            To Orgon.
Rest easy. You've had a scare, but thank God,
Gone are the days of injustice and fraud.
We live under a great prince who fosters
Love in our hearts and disdain for imposters.
He loves those in whom true piety sits
But he abhors the vices of hypocrites.
He recalled Tartuffe's notorious fame
For crimes committed under another name.
His record is a long and ugly one
That could fill volumes and still not be done.
The King has annulled, by royal decree
The deed of gift, thereby setting you free.

And finally, he pardons your offense
Of maintaining an exile's documents.
He shows how his subjects are protected
Even when the reward is least expected.
He recognizes true merit, as he should
And remembers, more than evil, the good.

                    DORINE
Heaven be praised!

                        MME. PERNELLE
                    At last, now I can breathe!

                    ELMIRE
Happy ending!

                    DORINE
                This is hard to believe!

                    ORGON
All right, traitor, there you go…

                    CLEANTE
                                    Brother, please,
Do not descend to such indignities.
Leave the wretch to his miserable life;
There's no need to add to his pain and strife.
Meanwhile, on your knees go before the King,
And thank him for mercy in everything.

                    ORGON
Yes, that's well said. So let us, on our knee,
Thank the King for his generosity.
Then, after that first duty has been done
We'll all gladly turn to another one,
And by a sweet marriage crown in Valere
The flame of love between this loving pair.

                End of Play

Introduction

"Lorsque vous peignez les hommes, il faut les peindre d'après la nature...Et vous n'avez rien fait si vous n'y faites reconnaitre les gens de votre siècle."
"When you are painting men, you must paint them according to nature...And you have done nothing if you do not make the people of your own time recognize themselves in them."

-- *Moliere*

The Tartuffe that we have today is Moliere's third version of the play. It was first performed on May 12, 1664 at Versailles and was immediately banned. The "pious" members of the court created a scandal out of Moliere's picture of false piety, loose family relations, and general social corruption. In 1667, the play was rewritten and performed under the new title of The Imposter, but this version was promptly banned also. Finally, in 1669, after the Peace of the Church was signed between Louis XIV and Pope Clement IX, Tartuffe was performed in its present version. In my opinion, the *deus ex machina* of the play's conclusion, which was adopted to appease and thank the king, is the classic example of how the government can hurt art when it interferes. The state and art are incompatible when the state has censorial superiority. Tartuffe as a play is very much weakened by its resolution, at least for modern audiences.

The most interesting and tragic thing about Moliere and Tartuffe is that in his personal life, Moliere was, at the moment of his death, a victim of the very hypocrisy against which he had so vehemently struggled. During a performance of Le Malade Imaginaire, his lungs collapsed; yet, he played the rest of the performance, took his bows, and was then rushed home. Bishop Bossuet refused, however, to give him the last rites of the Church, for "God was displaying his anger against Moliere."

It was one of the great exits of history.

"When an artist gives an interpretation of the works of another period and country, his interpretation is bound to belong to his own country and his own time. He can try to understand what is past and foreign, but it is utterly impossible to capture the spirit of three centuries ago in a foreign land. One day someone rang up Jouvet and criticized his production of a Moliere play, saying, 'Moliere would not have like that.' Jouvet answered, 'Have you got his phone number?' So a contemporary artist will give his interpretation of the past from the standpoint of today, on the basis either of traditions which are native to him, or of a knowledge, a feeling, an appreciation which he has acquired for the reality of past periods and other lands."

Miles Malleson

"Un œuvre d'art est un coin de la nature vue par un tempérament artiste."
"A work of art is a corner of nature seen by one artistic temperament."

Emile Zola

Moliere's <u>Tartuffe</u> is one of the best plays to come out of the French period of *classicisme* of the 17th century. It is a comedy in the true classic sense of the term. It is about hypocrisy, sensuality, self-centeredness, surface judgments, sex, love, romance, and reason – everything, in fact, that makes life worth living. <u>Tartuffe</u>, like most of Moliere's plays is an exaltation of the Aristotelian Golden Mean, which elucidates the effects and dangers of extremism and which extols the virtues of moderation. Although it is laced with a clever, pessimistic cynicism, reason, hope, and rational thought are triumphant.

If the *deus ex machina* of the denouement is the play's weak point, its strongest aspect is its characterizations. The actors and directors undertaking to make the characters live will find worlds of depth and meaning in them. Tartuffe is a corrupt, bigoted, hypocritical sensualist, deep and frightening in that he works on many different levels at once. Hypocrisy is his means to achieve his sensual pleasures. Possible the most fascinating of all comic character studies of evil, he uses the people from whom he wants something, and then he laughs in their faces as he finishes his rape. Elmire exemplifies virtue. Graceful, charming, and beautiful, she is also strong, rational, level, and reasonable. At the play's conclusion, she has a distinct promise of happiness with Orgon which she did not have before. Orgon is vain, pompous, and ludicrous in the extreme. He is also quite funny and quite likable. He may be said to be sympathetic in that he is so over-trusting that he becomes a gullible dupe. But he is, after all, the protagonist, and he is definitely a changed man when the ordeal is over. He is a new man, changed for the better, who has put behind him his former extremism which nearly destroyed him. <u>Tartuffe</u> is a serious comedy with serious implications; yet, when performed it is most effective when it induces loud belly laughs and guffaws (of self-recognition) from the audience.

Moliere's <u>Tartuffe</u>, as any professor of French will tell you, is for the ages. But it is also for us. Now.

Harold Dixon
Tucson, Arizona

The Comedy of Tartuffe as seen by Moliere

Here is a comedy about which there has been much ado, and which has been persecuted for a long time; and the people that it exposes have shown very well that they are more powerful in France than all of the others that I have exposed up to now. The Marquis, the Affected Young Ladies, the Cuckolds, and the Doctors have all suffered patiently while shown themselves on the stage, and they have even pretended to be entertained, along with everyone else, by the paintings that were made of them. The Hypocrites, however, have taken offense at the jokes aimed at them. At first, they were alarmed and found it strange that I had the impudence to show their grimaces and that I wanted to depict a profession in which so many honest men take part. It is a crime that they would not know how to forgive me, and they are all armed against my comedy with an appalling fury. Following their praiseworthy custom, they have covered their self-interests with God's cause; and Tartuffe, according to them, is a play that offends piety. It is, from beginning to end, full of abominations, and there is nothing in it that does not deserve hellfire.

That is what obliges me to defend myself. It is to the truly devout everywhere that I wish to justify myself on the disposition of my play; and I entreat them with all my heart not to condemn things before seeing them, to get rid of all prejudice, and not to serve the passions of those whose grimaces dishonor them.

If one takes the trouble to examine my comedy in good faith, one will no doubt see that my intentions in it are innocent throughout, and that it by no means proposes to satirize the things that must be revered. I have treated it with all the precautions that delicacy demands in the matter, and I have used all the art and taken all the pains that I could to distinguish very well the character of the Hypocrite from that of the truly Devout. To do this, I have used two entire acts to prepare the entrance of my scoundrel. He does not hold the audience in suspense about his character for a single moment. He is immediately seen for what he is by the marks which I gave him, and from beginning to end, he does not say a word, he does not do anything which does not paint the character of an evil man to the audience and which does not enlighten the character of the genuinely good man to which I oppose him.

Yet I know very well that, in response, these gentlemen try to insinuate that such matters should not be discussed in the theatre. But I ask them, with their permission, by what do they justify this fine maxim? It is a proposition that they only suppose, and one that they do not in any way prove. No doubt, it would not be hard to make them see that comedy, in the days of antiquity, originated from religion and was a part of the rituals; that the Spaniards, our neighbors, hardly celebrate any holiday without comedy playing some role; and that even among us, it owes its birth to the attentions of the Church.

If the function of Comedy is to correct the vices of men, I do not see why there should be any privileged ones.[2] In the Social Order, this one is of a much more dangerous consequence than all the others, and we have seen that the Theatre has a great virtue for correction. The finest traits of a serious story are more often less powerful than those of a satire, and nothing takes most men aback better than the painting of their defects. It is a big blow to vices to be exposed to everyone's laughter. Reprimands are easily endured, but mockery is not. We want very much to be evil, but no one wants to be ridiculed.

---

[2] See Don Juan: "Hypocrisy is a privileged vice," Act V, scene 2

I am reproached with having put expressions of piety in the mouth of my Impostor. Well, could I refrain from doing this and still portray well the character of a Hypocrite? It is enough, it seems to me, that I make known the criminal motives that make him say those things. One must approve of the comedy Tartuffe or condemn in general all comedies.

Let us finish with the words of a grand Prince concerning Tartuffe. Eight days after my comedy was banned, another play, entitled Scaramouche Ermite[3] was presented to the Court, and the King, when leaving, said to the grand Prince I mentioned, "I would very much like to know why the people who are so scandalized by Moliere's comedy do not say a word about this Scaramouche." To which the prince answered, "The reason for that is that the comedy of Scaramouche shows Heaven and religion, which these gentlemen do not care about at all; but Moliere's play shows them themselves. This is what they cannot endure."

Moliere

(Extracts from the Preface of the first edition of Tartuffe in 1669. Translated from the French by Harold Dixon)

---

[3] Scaramouche Ermite: a gross Italian farce

On Translating <u>Tartuffe</u>

Translations of any kind present many difficulties. Translations of plays present even more problems, because plays are meant to be seen, heard, and enjoyed live in the theatre, not read privately and savored in one's study. For a translation to work in the theatre, it must be true to the original, but the translator must strive to find up-to-date and idiomatic equivalents in the new language. One must never lose track of the fact that the words are going to spoken aloud by actors, and that the audience will get one chance to hear, understand, and grasp the significance of everything that is said. In this translation of Tartuffe, which is also slightly abridged, I have endeavored to create a "playable" version that will work in the theatre.

Eva LeGallienne, writing in her volume of translated Ibsen plays, wisely insists that the "foreign effect" of stilted language and unfamiliar expressions common in many play translations is to be avoided. For example, the William Archer versions of Ibsen are untrue, she says, because they distort the originals. Ibsen was an innovator and a genius, and Archer was a Victorian litterateur. His prose gives a sort of tempering gentility to Ibsen's fire and renders his plays dull. So, LeGallienne undertook new translations herself. LeGallienne insisted that translations are best when designed for production, as was her custom. A purely literary reworking of the play is often irrelevant and an injustice to the playwright.[4]

In his translations of Chekhov, Stark Young appears to be very much in accord with LeGallienne. He said that he wanted to write "Chekhov in English." Here are some examples that Young uses to show how a translator can distort meaning by changing the physical structure of the language of the original.

In the Russian she says, "You work too hard and have no time left to feel your own importance;" the translated young lady says, "You are overworked and you have not the leisure nor the desire to appreciate your own significance." In one translation, this same young lady, instead of saying that "evidently the play is not going on," soars into "apparently there's to be no continuation." And the remark that "everyone writes as he wants to and as he can" becomes "everyone writes in accordance with his desire and his capacity." Mr. Brooks Atkinson has exactly the right word for it when he speaks of how <u>opaque</u> some of the translations are that we have taken for granted.[5]

Young goes on to point out another problem in translating. There are many instances where the translator clearly prefers his/her own style to that of the original author.

For example, what the speech says in Russian is, "I fall always more and more behind, like a peasant missing his train, and the upshot is I can write only landscape and in all the rest I am false to the marrow of my bones." The translator undertakes to improve on that: "I am left behind them like a peasant missing his train at a station and finally I come back to the conclusion that all I am fit for is to describe landscapes, and that whatever else I attempt rings abominably false." If that seems unbelievable, it is less so perhaps than when

---

[4] Eva LeGallienne, <u>Six Plays by Ibsen</u>, pp. vii-ix.
[5] Stark Young, <u>Best Plays by Chekhov</u>, pp. viii-ix.

Sonia's lovely line in <u>Uncle Vanya</u>, "We shall see the whole sky all diamonds," is turned into "We shall see all Heaven lit with radiance."[6]

Young also stresses the importance of translating for the stage and not the written page:

"In <u>The Sea Gull</u>, Chekhov's actress shouts at the farm manager – and this is the exact order, number of words, and punctuation of her speech – "What horses? How should I know? What horses!" One translation has it, "What horses? How can I tell which?" That may seem a simple change but try and shout it. Or where the farm manager in a rage has to shout back at her, "You don't know what a farm means!" try shouting, "You don't know what the management of an estate involves!" Why such renderings are preferred to Chekhov's simple lines would be hard to explain."[7]

Donald Frame, a Moliere translator, has written about rhyming verse in the French originals. Many, but not all, of Moliere's plays are written in his version of the contemporary *alexandrin* verse. Frame states that "rhyme affects what Moliere says as well as the way he says it enough to make it worthwhile to use it in English."[8] James Rosenberg, in the introduction to his translation of <u>Tartuffe</u> states that the verse form of a poetic work is as much a part of its meaning as the dictionary equivalents of its words. <u>Tartuffe</u> in prose, then, would be like <u>Crime and Punishment</u> in blank verse. As translator Richard Wilbur puts it, "There is no question that words, when dancing within such patterns, are not their prosaic selves, but have a wholly different mood and meaning."[9]
  In other words, a play translation cannot be simply a United Nations version, where the accuracy is all. There is an artistic form, a style, and a structure that must be transferred as well. What follows are some examples from Moliere's play <u>The Misanthrope</u>, which will serve to illustrate this idea. The first is from a late 19th century translation by Henri Van Laun:

                    PHILINTE
I do not understand you in these abrupt moods, and
although we are friends, I am the first…

                    ALCESTE
I, your friend? Lay not that flattering unction to
your soul. I have until now professed to be so; but
after what I have just seen of you, I tell you
candidly that I am such no longer; I have no wish to
occupy a place in a corrupt heart.

                    PHILINTE
I am then very much to be blamed from your point of
view, Alceste?

---

[6] Young, <u>Chekhov</u>, p. ix.
[7] Young, <u>Chekhov</u>, p. x.
[8] Donald Frame, <u>Tartuffe and Other Plays by Moliere</u>, p. xiv.
[9] Richard Wilbur, <u>Tartuffe</u>, p.xi.

ALCESTE
```
To be blamed?  You ought to die from very shame.[10]
```

In my opinion, this is a dull version. The line, "Lay not that flattering unction to your soul" is especially bad, for it makes Moliere sound like a kind of second-rate echo of Shakespeare. Here is Richard Wilbur's version of the same section:

PHILINTE
```
These ugly moods of yours are not endearing;
Friends though we are, I really must insist…
```

ALCESTE
```
Friend? Friends, you say? Well, cross me off your list.
I've been your friend till now, as you well know;
But after what I saw a moment ago
I tell you flatly that our ways must part.
I wish no place in a dishonest heart.
```

PHILINTE
```
Why, what have I done, Alceste?  Is this quite just?
```

ALCESTE
```
My God, you ought to die of self-disgust.[11]
```

I believe that these contrasting examples serve to underscore the great responsibility that the play translator must shoulder. Moliere is France's greatest playwright, and it is crucial that we create English versions of his plays that capture the delight and essence of the originals.

The overall "feel" of Moliere's language is conversational. According to Donald Frame, Moliere's language is "plain, correct, functional…conversational."[12] In general, his language does not seem archaic in the original; therefore, it should not be so in English. Achieving a conversational tone, then, was of paramount importance to me in crafting this translation.

It was also useful for me to study Moliere's use of the *alexandrin* verse form, so named after a Twelfth Century poem called Le Roman d'Alexandre in which this form was used. It consists of couplets of alternating masculine and feminine rhymes of twelve syllables per line of verse. Rigidly defined by Boileau, it is the form used by Corneille and Racine for their tragedies such as Le Cid and Phedre, and it was used, in a somewhat modernized form, in the Nineteenth Century by Victor Hugo (Henani and Ruy Blas) and Edmond Rostand (Cyrano de Bergerac). The classical *alexandrin* was usually broken in the middle of the line, and no sentences were directly carried over from one line of verse to the next. As a result, much of the dialogue became "sing-songy" and was delivered in a declamatory manner. Moliere's *alexandrin* was not nearly so formal as that of Corneille or Racine. His verse lines are often "shared" by more than one character. In addition, he makes use of *enjambements*, or run-on lines, in which the sentence

---

[10] Henri Van Laun, The Dramatic Works of Moliere Rendered Into English, p. 193.

[11] Anthony Caputi, Baroque and Restoration Theatre, p. 53.

[12] Frame, Tartuffe, p. xiv

continues without a break at the end of the line of verse. Victor Hugo made use of similar *enjambements* in his plays, as did Shakespeare in his. Therefore, I freely made use of run on verse lines to help avoid the sing-song melody of a Hallmark card. I chose to use ten syllables per line in English rather than the twelve of the French original. I decided, largely because of my study of Shakespeare's use of iambic pentameter, that ten syllables per line better suits the words and rhythms of the English language. It is also easier to do than twelve!

I also worked for a great freedom of vocabulary, and I tried whenever possible to make the words simple, direct, and idiomatic. Here is an example. In French, Tartuffe says:

L'amour que nous attache aux beautés éternelles
N'etouffe pas en nous l'amour des temporelles.

This means: "The love which attaches us to eternal beauties does not stifle in us the love of earthly things." In Richard Wilbur's verse, this becomes:

A love of heavenly beauty does not preclude
A proper love for earthly pulchritude.[13]

In my translation, the verse is as follows:

To love eternal beauties far above
Does not mean I'm immune to earthly love.

The following example will serve to explain my use of the occasional vernacular term. In Act III, scene four, Damis says in French:

Le fourbe trop longtemps a gouverné mon père
Et desservi mes feux avec ceux de Valère.

I researched the literal meaning of the words. Desservir (the infinitive) means "to do an ill turn to," or "to harm, hurt, or be injurious to." Mes feux means, literally, "my fires" or ardor. Damis is a young hothead, so inserting a vernacular idiom in my translation, it becomes:

Too long that cheat has run father's affairs
Screwing up my love life, and poor Valere's

Concerning the cuts made from the original for this version, I hold that nothing essential is lacking, for the cuts are minimal. Most of them were inspired by comments in the Letter on the Impostor (Lettre Sur L'Imposteur) that describes the earlier version of Tartuffe entitled The Impostor (1667) which was banned. The French text I used mentioned in footnotes what parts of the script as we now know it were additions in 1669 to the earlier versions, such as the Police Officer's speech at the play's conclusion and Cleante's over-extended reasoning. In this version, these things are minimized in an attempt to give the play more of the flavor of what it might have been like before it was revised to please the King, the Court, and the Church.

---

[13] Wilbur, Tartuffe, p. 89